Such is]

A Play in Five Acts

Frank Wedekind

Alpha Editions

This edition published in 2024

ISBN : 9789364736442

Design and Setting By
Alpha Editions
www.alphaedis.com
Email - info@alphaedis.com

As per information held with us this book is in Public Domain.
This book is a reproduction of an important historical work. Alpha Editions uses the best technology to reproduce historical work in the same manner it was first published to preserve its original nature. Any marks or number seen are left intentionally to preserve its true form.

Contents

ACT I .... - 1 -
    Scene One—The Throne Room .... - 1 -
    Scene Two .... - 8 -

ACT II .... - 13 -
    Scene One. .... - 13 -
    Scene Two .... - 19 -

ACT III .... - 27 -
    Scene One. .... - 27 -
    Scene Two .... - 33 -
    Scene Three .... - 35 -

ACT IV .... - 44 -

ACT V .... - 59 -

ACT I

Scene One—The Throne Room.

FIRST SERVANT.

(*Leaning out of the window.*) They are coming! It will overtake us like the day of judgment!

SECOND SERVANT.

(*Rushing in through the opposite door.*) Do you know that the King is taken?

FIRST SERVANT.

Our King a captive?

SECOND SERVANT.

Since early yesterday! The dogs have thrown him into prison!

FIRST SERVANT.

Then we had better scamper away, or they will treat us as if we were the beds upon which he has debauched their children!

(*The servants rush out. The room becomes filled with armed workmen of various trades, heated and blood-splashed from combat.*)

PIETRO FOLCHI.

(*Steps from their midst.*) Fellow-citizens!—The byways of Perugia are strewn with the corpses of our children and our brothers. Many of you have a pious wish to give your beloved dead a fitting resting place.—Fellow-citizens! First we must fulfill a higher duty. Let us do our part as quickly as possible, so that the dead shall have perished, not solely for their bravery, but for the lasting welfare of their native-land! Let us seize the moment! Let us give our state a constitution which, in future, will protect her children from the assassin's weapons and insure her citizens the just reward of their labors!

THE CITIZENS.

Long live Pietro Folchi!

ANDREA VALORI.

Fellow-citizens! Unless we decide at once upon our future form of government, we shall only be holding this dearly captured place for our enemies until we lose it again. We are holding the former King in custody in prison; the patricians, who supported themselves in idleness by the sweat of our brows, are in flight toward neighboring states. Now, I ask you, fellow-citizens, shall we proclaim our state the Umbrian Republic, as has been done in Florence, in Parma, and in Siena?

THE CITIZENS.

Long live Freedom! Long live Perugia! Long live the Umbrian Republic!

PIETRO FOLCHI.

Let us proceed without delay to elect a podesta! Here are tables and styles in plenty. Let each one write the name of the man whom he considers best fitted to guide the destiny of the state and to defend the power we have gained from our enemies.

THE CITIZENS.

Long live our podesta, Pietro Folchi! Long live the Republic of Perugia!

ANDREA VALORI.

Fellow-citizens! Let there be no precipitate haste at this hour! It is necessary to strengthen so the power we have won that they cannot prevail against us as long as we live. Would we succeed if we made Umbria a republic? Under the shelter of republican liberty, the sons of the banished nobles would use the vanity of our daughters to bind us again in chains while we slept unsuspectingly at night! Look at Florence! Look at Siena! Is not liberty in those states only the cloak of the most dissolute despotism, which is turning their citizens to beggars? Perugia grew in power and prosperity under her kings, until the sceptre passed into the hands of a fool and a wastrel. Let us raise the worthiest of us up to his throne. Then we who stand here exhausted from the conflict, will become the future aristocracy and the lords of the land; only then can we enjoy in lasting peace our hard won prerogatives.

THE CITIZENS.

Long live the king! Long live Pietro Folchi!

A FEW VOICES.

Long live Freedom!

THE CITIZENS.

(Louder.) Long live our king, Pietro Folchi! Long live King Pietro!

A FEW CITIZENS.

(*Leaving the room angrily.*) We did not shed our blood for this. Down with slavery! Long live Freedom!

THE CITIZENS.

Hurrah for King Pietro!

PIETRO FOLCHI.

(*Mounting the throne.*) Called to it by your choice, I mount this throne and name myself King of Umbria! The dissatisfied who have separated from our midst with the cry of "freedom" are no less our enemies than the idle nobles who have turned their backs to our walls. I shall keep a watchful eye on them, as they fought on our side only in the hope of plundering in the ruins of our beloved city. Where is my son Filipo?

FILIPO FOLCHI.

(*Stepping from out the press.*) What is your will, my father?

KING PIETRO.

From the wounds above your eyes, I see that you did not shun death yesterday or today! I name you commander of our war forces. Post our loyal soldiers at the ten gates of the city, and order the drum to beat in the market place for recruits. Perugia must be armed for an expedition to its frontiers in the shortest possible time. You will be answerable to me for the life of every citizen and responsible for the inviolate safety of all property. Now bring the former king of Umbria forth from his prison. It is proper that none save I announce to him his sentence.

FILIPO.

Your commands shall be observed punctually. Long live King Pietro! (*Exit.*)

KING PIETRO.

Where is my son-in-law, Andrea Valori?

ANDREA VALORI.

(*Stepping forward.*) Here, my king, at your command!

KING PIETRO.

I name you treasurer of the Kingdom of Umbria. You and my cousin, Giullio Diaceto, together with our celebrated jurist, Bernardo Ruccellai, whose persuasive words abroad have more than once preserved our city from bloodshed; you three shall be my advisors in the discharge of affairs of state. (*After the three summoned have come forward.*) Seat yourselves beside me. (*They do so.*) I can only fulfill the high duty of ruling others if the most able men in the state will enlist their lives in my service. And now, let the others go to bury the victims of this two days' conflict. To show that they did not die in vain for the welfare of their brothers and children, let this be a day of mourning and earnest vigilance.

(*All leave the room save King Pietro, the Councillors and several guards. Then the captive King is led in by Filipo Folchi and several armed men.*)

THE KING.

Who is bold enough to dare bring us here at the bidding of these disloyal knaves?!

KING PIETRO.

According to the provision of our laws, the royal power in Umbria fell to you as eldest son of King Giovanni. You have used your power to degrade the name of a king with roisterers and courtesans. You chose banquets, masquerades and hunting parties, by which you have dissipated the treasures of the state and made the country poor and defenseless, in preference to every princely duty. You have robbed us of our daughters, and your deeds have been the most corrupting example to our sons. You have lived as little for the state's welfare as for your own. You accomplished only the downfall of your own and our native land.

THE KING.

To whom is the butcher speaking?

FILIPO FOLCHI.

Silence!

THE KING.

Give me back my sword!

ANDREA VALORI.

Put him in chains! He is raving!

THE KING.

Let the butcher speak further.

KING PIETRO.

Your life is forfeited and lies in my hands. But I will suspend sentence of death if in legal document you will relinquish in my favor, and in favor of my heirs, your claim and that of your kin to the throne, and acknowledge me as your lord, your rightful successor and as the ruler of Umbria.

THE KING.

(*Laughs boisterously.*) Ha, ha, ha! Ask of a carp lying in the pan to cease to be a fish! That this worm has our life in his power proves indeed that princes are not gods, because, like other men, they are mortal. The lightning, too, can kill; but he who is born a king does not die like an ordinary mortal! Let one of these artisans lay hands upon us, if his blood does not first chill in his veins. Then he shall see how a king dies!

KING PIETRO.

You are a greater enemy to yourself than your deadliest foes can possibly be. Although you will not abdicate, we will be mild, in thankful remembrance of the blessed rule of King Giovanni, whose own son you are, and banish you now and forever from the confines of the Umbrian States, under penalty of death.

THE KING.

Banish! Ha, ha, ha! Who in the world will banish the King! Shall fear of death keep him from the land of which Heaven appointed him the ruler? Only an artisan could hold life so dear and a crown so cheap!——Ha, ha, ha! These pitiable fools seem to imagine that when a crown is placed upon a butcher he becomes a king! See how the paunch-belly grows pale and shivers up there, like a cheese flung against the wall! Ha, ha, ha! How they stare at us, the stupid blockheads, with their moist dogs' eyes, as if the sun had fallen at their feet!

PRINCESS ALMA.

(*Rushes in, breaking through the guards at the door. She is fifteen years old, is clad in rich but torn garments and her hair is disheveled.*) Let me pass! Let me go to my father! Where is my father? (*Sinking down before the King and embracing his knees.*) Father! Have I you again, my dearly beloved father?

THE KING.

(*Raising her.*) So I hold you unharmed in my arms once more, my dearest treasure! Why must you come to me with your heartrending grief just at this moment when I had almost stamped these bloodthirsty hounds beneath my feet again!

ALMA.

Then let me die with you! To share death with you would be the greatest happiness, after what I have lived through in the streets of Perugia these last two days! They would not let me come to you in prison, but now you are mine again! Remember, my father, I have no one else in the world but you!

THE KING.

My child, my dear child, why do you compel me to confess before my murderers how weak I am! Go! I have brought my fate upon myself, let me bear it alone. These men will confirm it that you may expect more compassion and better fortune from my bitterest enemies than if you cling now to your father, broken by fate.

ALMA.

(*With greatest intensity.*) No, do not say that! I beseech you do not speak so again! (*Caressingly.*) Only remember that it is not yet decided that they murder us. And if we had rather die together than be parted who in the world can harm us then!

KING PIETRO.

(*Who during this scene has quietly come to an agreement with his councillors, turning to the King.*) The city of Perugia will give your daughter the most careful education until her majority; and then bestow upon her a princely dower; if she will promise to give her hand in marriage to my son, Filipo Folchi, who will be my successor upon this throne.

THE KING.

You have heard, my child? The throne of your father is open to you!

ALMA.

O my God, how can you so scoff at your poor child!

KING PIETRO.

(*To the King.*) As for you, armed men under the command of my son shall conduct you, within this hour, to the confines of this country. Have a care that you do not take so much as a step within our land hereafter, or your head shall fall by the hand of the executioner in the market place of Perugia!

(*Filipo Folchi has the King and the Princess, clinging close to her father, led off by men-at-arms. He is about to follow them, when his arm is seized by Benedetto Nardi, who rushes in breathless with rage.*)

BENEDETTO NARDI.

Have I caught you, scoundrel! (*To King Pietro.*) This son of yours, Pietro Folchi, in company with his drunken comrades, chased my helpless child through the streets of the city yesterday evening, and was about to lay hands on her when two of my journeymen, attracted by her cries, put the scoundrels to flight with their clubs. The wretch still carries the bloody mark above his eyes!

KING PIETRO.

(*In anger.*) Defend yourself, my son!

FILIPO FOLCHI.

He speaks the truth.

KING PIETRO.

Back to the shop with you! Must I see my rule disgraced on its first day by my own son in most impious fashion! The law shall work its greatest hardship upon you! Afterward you shall stay in the butcher shop until the citizens of Perugia kneel before me and beg me to have pity on you! Put him in chains!

(*The mercenaries who led out the King return with Alma. Their leader throws himself on his knees before the throne.*)

THE MERCENARY.

O Sire, do not punish your servants for this frightful misfortune! As we were leading the King just here before the portal across the bridge of San Margherita, a company of our comrades marched past and pressed us against the coping. The prisoner seized that opportunity to leap into the flood swollen by the rain. We needed all our strength to prevent this maiden from doing likewise, and when I was about to leap after the prisoner, the raging waves had long engulfed him.

KING PIETRO.

His life is not the most regrettable sacrifice of these bloody days! Hundreds of better men have fallen for him. (*To the Councillors.*) Let the child be taken to the Urseline nuns and kept under most careful guard. (*Rising.*) The sitting of the counsel is closed.

ALL PRESENT.

Long live King Pietro!

Scene Two

A highway along the edge of a forest.
(*The King and Princess Alma, both clad as beggars.*)

THE KING.

How long have I been dragging you from place to place while you begged for me?

ALMA.

Rest yourself, Father; you will be in better spirits afterward.

THE KING.

(*Sits down by the wayside.*) Why did not the raging waves swallow me that evening! Then everything would have been over long ago!

ALMA.

Did you leap over the side of the bridge to put an end to your life? I thought what strength resided in your arms and that the rushing waters would help you to liberty. Without this faith how should I have had the courage to escape from the convent and from the city?

THE KING.

Below us here lies the rich hunting grounds where I have often ridden hawking with my court. You were too young to accompany us.

ALMA.

Why will you not leave this little land of Umbria, my father! The world is so large! In Siena, in Modena, your friends dwell. They would welcome you with joy, and at last your dear head would be safe.

THE KING.

You offer me much, my child! Still, I beg of you not to keep repeating this question. Just in this lies my fate: If I were able to leave this land, I should not have lost my crown. But my soul is ruled by desires which I cannot relinquish, even to save my life. As king, I believed myself safe enough from the world to live my dreams without danger. I forgot that the king, the peasant and every other man, must live only to preserve his station and to defend his estate, unless he would lose both.

ALMA.

Now you are scoffing at yourself, my father!

THE KING.

That is the way of the world!——You think I am scoffing at myself?—— That, at least, might be something for which men would contribute to our support. As I offer myself to them now I am of no use. Either I offend them by my arrogance and pride, which are in ridiculous contrast to my beggar's rags, or my courteous demeanor makes them mistrustful, as none of them succeeds by simple modesty. How my spirit has debased itself during these six months, in order to fit itself to their ways and methods! But everything I learned as hereditary prince of Umbria is valueless in their world, and everything which is of worth in their world I did not learn as a prince. But if I succeed in jesting at my past, my child, who knows but what we may find again a place at a richly decked table! When the pork butcher is raised to the throne there remains no calling for the king save that of court fool.

ALMA.

Do not enrage yourself so in your fatigue, my father. See, you must take a little nap! I will look for fresh water to quench your thirst and cool your fevered brow.

THE KING.

(*Laying down his head.*) Thank you, my child.

ALMA.

(*Kissing him.*) My dear father! (*Exit.*)

THE KING.

(*Rises.*) How I have grown to love this beautiful land since I have slunk about it at the risk of my life! ——Even the worst disaster always brings good with it. Had I not cared so little for my brave people of Perugia and Umbria, had I not shown myself to them only at carnivals and in fancy dress, God knows, but I might have been recognized long ago! Here comes one of them now!

(*A landed proprietor comes up the road.*)

THE KING.

God greet you, sir! Can you not give me work on your estate?

THE LANDED PROPRIETOR.

You might find much to recompense your work on my estate, but, thank God, my house is guarded by fierce wolf hounds. And here, you see, I carry a hunting knife, which I can use so well that I should not advise you to come a step nearer me!

THE KING.

Sir, you have no guarantee from Heaven that you may not be compelled at some time to beg for work in order not to go hungry.

THE LANDED PROPRIETOR.

Ha, ha, ha! He who works in order not to go hungry, he is the right kind of worker for me! First comes work and then the hunger. Let him who can live without work starve rather today than tomorrow!

THE KING.

Sir, you must have had wiser teachers than I!

THE LANDED PROPRIETOR.

I should hope so! What have you learned?

THE KING.

The trade of war.

THE LANDED PROPRIETOR.

Thank God, under the rule of King Pietro, whom Heaven long preserve to us, there is little use for that in Umbria any longer. City and country enjoy peace, and at last we live in concord with neighboring states.

THE KING.

Sir, you will find me of use for any work on your estate.

THE LANDED PROPRIETOR.

I will think over the matter. You appear a harmless fellow. I am on my way to my nephew, who has a large house and family at Todi. I am coming back this afternoon. Wait for me here at this spot. Possibly I will take you with me then. (*Exit.*)

THE KING.

"Let him who can live without work starve." What old saws this vermin cherished to endure his miserable existence! And I?———I cannot even feed my child! A lordship was given me by Heaven such as only one in a million can have! And I cannot even give my child food!———My kind father made every hour of the day a festival for me by means of joyous companions, by the wisest, teachers, by a host of devoted servants, and my child must shiver with cold and sleep under the hedges by the highway! Have pity on her, O God, and blot her love for miserable me out of her heart! Let happen to me then whatever will, I will bear it lightly!

ALMA.

(*Rushes out of the bushes with her hair tumbling down.*) Father! Jesu Maria! My father! Help!

THE KING.

(*Clasping her in his arms.*) What is it, child?

A VAGABOND.

(*Who has followed the maiden, comes forward and stops.*) Ah!—How could I know another had her!

THE KING.

(*Rushes upon him with uplifted stick.*) Hence, you dirty dog!

THE VAGABOND.

I a dirty dog! What are you, then?

THE KING.

(*Striking him.*) That am I!—And that!—And that!

(*The vagabond seeks refuge in flight.*)

ALMA.

(*Trembling in her father's arms.*) O Father, I was leaning over the spring when that man sprang at me!

THE KING.

(*Breathing hard.*) Calm yourself, my child

ALMA.

My poor father! That I, instead of being able to help you, must still need your help!

THE KING.

Today I shall take you back to Perugia. Will throw you at King Pietro's feet——

ALMA.

Oh, do not let me hear of that again! Can I leave you when death threatens you daily?

THE KING.

It would be better for you to wear man's clothes, instead of a woman's dress, in the future. It is marvel enough that Providence has protected you until today from the horrors that threaten you in our wanderings! You will be safer in man's clothes. A countryman just passed this way. When he comes back he will take me with him and give me work on his place.

ALMA.

Will you really seek again to put yourself in the service of those so abyssmally beneath you?

THE KING.

What are you saying, my child! Why are they below me?——Besides, it is not quite certain that he will find me worthy of his work. If he asks me to go with him, then follow us, so that I can turn my place under his roof over to you at night.

ALMA.

No, no! You must not suffer hardship on my account. Have I deserved that of you?

THE KING.

Do you know, my child, that if I had not had you with me, my treasure, as guardian angel, I should very probably be hanging today on a high gallows for highway robbery?——(*He sits down again by the road-side.*) And now, let us tarry here in patient expectation of the all-powerful man whose return will decide whether our desire to live in communion with mankind is to be fulfilled.

ACT II

Scene One.

THE WORKSHOP OF A LADIES' TAILOR.

(The King, in journeyman's clothes, sits cross-legged on a table, working on a woman's gown of rich material. Master Pandolfo bustles into the room.)

MASTER PANDOLFO.

Early to work, Gigi! Early to work! Bravo, Gigi!

THE KING.

The cock has crowed, Master!

MASTER PANDOLFO.

Now shake me the other fellows awake. One can work better in company than alone, Gigi! *(Takes the dress out of his hands.)* See here, Gigi! *(He tears the dress.)* Rip! What's the use of early to bed and early to rise if the stitches don't hold? And the button-holes, Gigi! Did the rats help you with them? I worked for Her Majesty Queen Amelia when her husband was still making mortadella and salmi. Am I to lose her custom now because of your botching? Hey, Gigi?

THE KING.

If my work shames you, turn me out!

MASTER PANDOLFO.

How rude, Gigi! Do you think you are still tending pigs at Baschi? Forty years on your back and nothing learned! Go packing out of my house and see where you will find your food, then, you vagabond!

THE KING.

(Rises and collects the scraps.) I'll take you at your word, Master!

MASTER PANDOLFO.

What the devil, madcap; can't you take a joke? Can I show more love toward my 'prentice than I do when I give him the work which usually the master does? Since you have been with me haven't I allowed you to cut all the garments? The devil take me that I cannot catch the knack of your cutting! But the ladies of Perugia say, "Master Pandolfo, since the old apprentice has been working for you, your work has a genteel cut." But what's the use of a genteel cut if the young ladies tear the stitches out as they dance? You'll never be a journeyman, Gigi, unless you learn to sew. My dear, sweet Gigi, don't you see that I only want what's best for you?

THE KING.

Good, Master Pandolfo, I'll stay with you if from now on, in addition to my keep, you will pay me thirty soldi more a week.

MASTER PANDOLFO.

I'll promise you that, Gigi! As true as I stand here, I'll promise you that!——Thirty soldi you want?——Yes, yes! The gown for her Majesty, the Queen, must be ready sewed by noon. Therefore, be industrious, Gigi! Always industrious! (*Exit.*)

(*The King dimes a long breath after Master Pandolfo leaves the room, and then sits down to his work again. After a while, Princess Alma puts her head in through the window.*)

ALMA.

Are you alone, Father?

THE KING.

(*Springing up joyfully.*) My treasure!

(*Alma vanishes and immediately after comes in through the door. She is dressed as a boy in a dark, neat suit of clothes.*)

THE KING.

The master is upstairs with his morning dram, and the journeymen are still asleep. The moments I have with you, my child, indemnify my soul for the days of dull routine. What affectionate conversations I hold with you, and how lovingly and understandingly you answer me! Do not forsake me! It is a new crime I commit in asking this of you; but see, I am a weak man!

ALMA.

Things will soon be better with us now, Father. The old notary, whose errand-boy I became two months ago, already lets me copy all his documents. Next week he is going to take me to court with him, in order that I may take down the case instead of him.——O my father, if only the death sentence which, now that we are in Perugia again, places you in greater danger than ever before, could be lifted from your head!——My feminine ignorance of politics prevents me conjecturing whether they will raise you to the throne again. But they should honor you as more than a king. There must be something godlike about you when, in spite of your degradation, you are able to fill one with happiness as you do me! What a wealth of happiness you would have to give if your fetters were removed. Thousands then would contend for you, and you would no longer envy any king the weight of his crown!

THE KING.

Do not talk further about me. I must wait in obscurity until my hour is come.——But you, my child, do you not feel deadly unhappy under the burden of your work?——Isn't your master disagreeable when he needs someone upon whom to vent his bad temper?

ALMA.

But don't you see what good spirits I am in, Father? The people I serve know how to value education and culture. You, on the contrary, must live with a brood of men whose daily habits must torment your soul, even without their knowledge or desire. I see you grind your teeth at this or that retort. I see how your throat contracts with disgust at mealtimes. Oh, forgive my words! They are unmindful of your smarting wounds.

THE KING.

(*Whimsically.*) Only think, my child, the result of these unusual circumstances is that I am cherished by Master Pandolfo as his most industrious worker. At Baschi, where I tended cattle, I made a shed behind the stables my sleeping place. I used to lie there every morning on my back, following my dreams until the sun stood over me in the zenith. That's the reason the farmer discharged me. Here I sleep with three common fellows, and, therefore, am the first to rise and the last to go to bed. Personally, I do not sleep as well in the company of men as I do in the company of beasts. I never dreamed such an industrious worker was concealed within me! Work serves me as a kind of refuge. And then the beautiful lines of the heavy velvet, the sheen of the gold brocade! They refresh my soul and I long for them as for a vivifying drink. And then Master Pandolfo's insight discovered in me at once a gift which astonishes me highly, and which, to be can-did, I could not give up lightly. He found I was better able than any of his workmen, better able than himself even, to cut the stuff for the ladies' dresses so as to bring out the figure to the best advantage. For example, that doublet you wear I should have cut quite differently than did that miserable botcher whose shears were not worthy to touch such splendid cloth.

ALMA.

Oh, silence, Father! How can you jest so callously at your unhappy fate!

THE KING.

(*Passionately.*) Do not mock me with flattery, my child! Fate jests at me and not I at it!

ALMA.

(*Soothingly.*) Beloved father, you remain a king, no matter what you must do in this world.

THE KING.

In your loving heart, yes! And, therefore, your father, with loving despotism, opposes your life's happiness by crowding out of your heart that longing for a man which must be awakening in you at your age. Your father's egotistical folly has lost you rank and property, now it deprives you of the highest rights of life—those which the creatures of the wilderness share with mankind and which may make existence in a hut, as well as on a throne, a gift of the gods! What madness made me test my strength against the flood of the San Margherita brook, instead of invading Umbria by war, setting the city on fire at its four corners and snatching the crown with my own hands from the glowing ruins!——But that was only the continuation of past folly!

ALMA.

(*Weeping.*) Heaven have mercy on my foolish soul! How was it possible for me so to grieve you!

THE KING.

In misfortune people hurt each other without knowledge or desire, just as truly as in happiness each one brings joy to the other unwittingly. Do not make him who is judged suffer for it. You must go, my child; I hear the workmen shouting and tramping about upstairs.

ALMA.

(*Kissing him.*) Tomorrow morning early! (*Exit.*)

(*The King takes up his work. Then the three journeymen come in, and, sitting down on separate tables on the other side of the room, prepare for work.*)

MICHELE.

Gigi, if you get up before cockcrow again I'll break your nose the next night while you sleep. Then go to the women and see if you can succeed with them!

THE KING.

It would please you well to attack a sleeping man. But take care of your own bones at it, or perhaps you might not rise at all the next day!

NOE.

Well said, Gigi! Tell us quickly more of your war-like deeds, that we may be afraid of you.

THE KING.

I haven't time. If your ears itch for tales of heroic deeds, tell how you stole the parson's geese at Bavagna.

BATTISTA.

Our patron saint defend us! Usually, you are as tame and sneaking as if your nail had never crushed a louse, and today you would like to spit all three of us at once on your needle.

THE KING.

Let me be in peace, then! A hollow tooth is hurting me. That's the reason I left the sleeping room so early.

NOE.

Tell the truth, Gigi! Wasn't the page here just now who brings you the glowing love letters from the lady for whom you cut the yellow silk dress?

THE KING.

Do I concern myself with your love letters?

MICHELE.

You concern yourself with entirely different things! You get up right after midnight to practice being a lickspittle and a trimmer! You get the master to give you the journeymen's work and divide the apprentice's work among us! You are a pest in the house!

BATTISTA.

Apprentice, bring us the morning soup!

(*The King leaves the workroom.*)

NOE.

He's lacking in the upper story; I am sorry for him. He must have been some sort of bootcleaner for a gentleman of quality. That moved his brain out of place in his skull.

BATTISTA.

Did you ever see a soldier who would let himself be kicked about so by journeymen tailors?

NOE.

My mother was a country girl; I tell that to anybody who asks me; I don't act as if I had been bed servant to the Holy Father!

MICHELE.

I'll tell you why the lad is so stupid. Each of us has knocked about the world, often with not enough to eat. But if he opens his mouth out comes a stream of curses profane enough to turn one's stomach. Earth is ashamed at having brought forth such a monster; then Heaven is ashamed to have let its light fall upon him; then Hell is ashamed that it has not yet swallowed him! You will see!

(*The King returns with four wooden, spoons and a pot of soup, which he sets before the journeymen.*)

MICHELE.

Get out, you beast! You can lick our spoons when we have had enough!

THE KING.

(*Strives with himself, seeking to master his anger, then strikes his brow.*) Oh, a curse upon this king who hinders me from allowing myself to be thrashed by this rascal! Oh, a curse upon the king who hinders me crushing this rascal, whom I understand better than he understands me! Oh, a curse upon the king who hinders me from being a man like other men! Oh a triple curse upon the king!

(*The journeymen spring up in horror.*)

MICHELE.

Did you hear? He cursed the king! He cursed the king!

BATTISTA AND NOE.

(*Together.*) He has cursed the king!

MICHELE.

Seize him! Hold him fast!———Master Pandolfo!———Master Pandolfo!———Knock in his teeth!

MASTER PANDOLFO.

(*Rushing in.*) Get to work, lads! Why are you fighting so early in the morning? Are you mad?

THE JOURNEYMEN.

(*Holding the King by the arms.*) He has cursed the king!———"Curse the king!" he cried! "A triple curse upon the king!"

THE KING.

(*Submitting indifferently to force.*) A triple curse upon the king! Then let the king's head fall under the headsman's axe.

THE JOURNEYMEN.

Listen to him, Master Pandolfo!

THE KING.

(*To himself.*) My poor child!

MASTER PANDOLFO.

Bind his hands behind his back! Cursing our dear, good King Pietro! "Let King Pietro's head fall under the headsman's axe!" Bring ropes! Take the dog to court! This vagabond will lose me by best customers! The head of King Pietro, who pays his bills more promptly than any king before him!

Scene Two.

THE COURT ROOM.

(*The presiding judge and two associates sit at the middle table; the attorney-general for the crown occupies a raised seat to the right; the counsel for the defense occupies a similar seat to the left. Further forward, to the right, is the clerk of the court, with Princess Alma as his amanuensis. She has the court records in front of her. Forward, on the left, are halberdiers guarding the door to the adjoining room. The back of the hall is filled with spectators.*)

THE PRESIDING JUDGE.

I open the session in the name of his exalted Majesty, the king.——
According to his request, I grant the privilege of speaking first to the
counsel for the prosecution, Signor Silvio Andrevitti, Doctor of Canonical
and Civil Law and Attorney-General for the Crown.

THE ATTORNEY-GENERAL.

Under the rule of our sublime and beloved King Pietro, it has become the
custom in our city of Perugia to permit the citizen to be present in court
during a trial, in order to strengthen his confidence in the unshakable
incorruptibility of our judgments. In view of the offence which is to be
tried here today, I venture to suggest to the court that the spectators here
assembled be excluded from our session, in order that they may be
protected from looking too deeply into the degradation of human nature.

THE PRESIDING JUDGE.

The well-considered suggestion of the honorable Attorney-General shall be
followed.

(*The halberdiers, with crossed pikes, force the spectators quietly out of the hall.*)

THE PRESIDING JUDGE.

Our sublime King Pietro has made the wise and just provision that any
poor defendant, no matter what his nationality, be supplied with an
advocate at the cost of the state. The worthy Signor Corrado Ezzelino,
master and doctor of both civil and canonical law, has declared himself
ready to serve in this capacity today. Now, I grant the privilege of speaking,
at his special request, to our worthy clerk of the court, Signor Matteo Nerli.

THE CLERK OF THE COURT.

Honorable and wise judges, a cramp which lames my right hand, the result
of long years of untiring industry in the service of the law, does not permit
me the honor of taking down the minutes of to-day's session unassisted. By
my side you see my apprenticed clerk, a lad who has awakened my
affection, and who, despite his youth, has shown an unusual love of the
law. I ask that he be permitted to keep the minutes, under the direction and
supervision of his master.

THE PRESIDING JUDGE.

Your wish is granted, blaster Matteo. The witnesses who were called for today's session have all appeared in person. Conduct the defendant thither.

(*The halberdiers bring in the King from the neighboring room. Princess Alma startles at
sight of him, but collects herself and arranges her writing materials.*)

THE PRESIDING JUDGE.

You call yourself Ludovicus and were employed formerly in tending cattle at Baschi. You are accused of the *crimen læsæ majestatis*, which was visited with severe penalties in the imperishable code of our great predecessors, the ancient Romans; the crime of injuring majesty, or, in other words, the insult to the holy person of the king. Do you acknowledge yourself guilty of this offence?

THE KING.

Yes.

THE CLERK OF THE COURT.

(*To Alma.*) He said "yes." Write it down, my lad; write it down accurately!

THE PRESIDING JUDGE.

According to the unanimous testimony of four unprejudiced witnesses, your words were, "A triple curse upon the king! Let the king's head fall under the headsman's axe!"

THE KING.

Those were my words.

THE CLERK OF THE COURT.

"Those were my words!" Joseph and Mary, a blot! Lad, has the devil gotten into you today?

THE PRESIDING JUDGE.

What have you to advance in your own behalf?

THE KING.

Nothing.

MICHELE.

He has nothing to advance! Did you hear? He has nothing to advance!

MASTER PANDOLFO.

He spat out his terrible curse in miserable revenge against me! He wanted to bring my business and my whole family into disrepute.

THE PRESIDING JUDGE.

Silence on the witness bench!——Now, what have you to say in your own defense?

THE KING.

Nothing.———Next to the majesty of God, the majesty of the king stands highest in this world. The majesty of God suffers as little from human curses as the majesty of the king. Can the majesty of God be dimmed by vulgar humanity saying, "We believe in you no longer"? Can the majesty of the king be dimmed by people saying, "We will obey no longer"? Who would assert that as possible?———God wandered in lowly form upon this earth, and the rabble believed it had put him to death. And so the rabble may believe it has banished the king; he remains where he was. If they call to him, "Let your head fall under the headsman's axe," it does him no harm. Therefore, although next to blaspheming against God, blaspheming against the king is the most execrable crime—a crime of which my words have made me guilty, as I acknowledge openly———it appears to me that the matter should be such an indifferent and trifling affair to the king that he should not need to revenge it. At the same time, it seems to me too frightful for the rabble to presume to be able ever to atone for it. The rabble, indeed, possesses no higher power than that over life and death, and, indeed, cannot know whether the miserable sinner would not welcome death, no matter how painful, as a liberation from a thousand sorrows. These, therefore, are the reasons why I hold that the judges before whom I now stand can execute no punishment upon me for my crime. (*General murmur of dissent.*) Now, let me, wise and honorable judges, name the grounds which make it your holy duty to judge me according to the greatest severity of the law.

NOE.

I told you the fellow was completely crazy!

THE PRESIDING JUDGE.

(*To the witness bench.*) Silence! (*To the King.*) Speak further.

THE KING.

The majesty of the king, as I have proved commensurate to human reason, can receive no injury from my words. But, unfortunately, next to faith in the All-Goodness of Providence, faith in the majesty of the king is the highest and holiest possession of the common people. That which the sons of earth have known since all time as eternal truths, against which none, be he master or slave, sins unpunished, that stands under God's holy protection. Everything which they value, everything that affects their property and the prosperity of their daily work, that they enjoy with childish confidence in their king's protection. In their king the common people recognize the likeness of their own fortune, and who smirches this likeness robs them of the courage to work and of peace by night. I am far more guilty of this crime than human justice fathoms. It is impossible for the punishment hanging over me to approach the weight of my crime. Even should it cost my life, let it be what you will, I shall accept it from the hands of you judges as a grace of God.

THE PRESIDING JUDGE.

The grace of your lord, our dear and blessed king, has placed a learned advocate at your side. The honorable Signor Corrado Ezzelino, Master and Doctor of Civil and Canonical Law, may address the court.

THE ADVOCATE FOR THE DEFENSE.

(*Rising.*) My exalted, righteous, worthy and honorable judges, permit me first to speak a word concerning our brave and honest fellow-citizen, the master-tailor Casare Pandolfo. We see him here today on the witness bench deeply bowed down as the result of the abominable crime which has taken place under his roof. We all of us recognize the staunchness of his principles; we all—all of us here assembled—know the excellence of his work. I believe myself able, therefore, to assure Master Pandolfo, in the name of all of us, that not one of us would think of associating him, even in the slightest degree, with the frightful crime which happened under his roof.——Now, concerning the defendant, whom it is my sad duty to defend: Apparently, he is an entirely disreputable scamp, more worthy of our deepest scorn than of being judged in the normal fashion according to the wise provision of the Roman code. Permit, O judges, the words of the text, "Thou shalt not cast thy pearls before swine," to be followed in the case of this outcast from our dear commonweal. Because of his unexampled spiritual and moral degeneracy, it would be impossible for the defendant to know how to appreciate at its true worth the honor done him by weighing his case in the scales of justice; therefore, I request you, wise and honorable judges, in order not to belittle the dignity of our calling, to let the punishment rest at flogging. Should punishment by flogging appear inadequate, wise and honorable judges, possibly punishment by flogging might be augmented by three days' exposure in the pillory in the market place of Perugia.

THE PRESIDING JUDGE.

I grant the floor to the Attorney-General, our worthy Signor Silvio Andreotti, Doctor of Civil and Canonical Law.

THE ATTORNEY-GENERAL.

(*Who during the whole proceedings has been groaning, yawning and wriggling about in his seat.*) Honorable judges! As the worthy Signor Corrado Ezzelino has rightly and forcibly expressed it in his excellent defence, the defendant is a disreputable scamp, an outcast from our dear human community, an individual of unexampled moral degeneracy, in whom I cannot deny there is a certain mental craftiness, or, to speak more plainly, a certain peasant's cunning. His own words which he has spoken here are evidence of this peasant's cunning, as is also the fact that, with the intention of confusing our power of judgment, by creating a favorable impression, he has not attempted to deny his deed. When, however, an individual from the lowest depths of human degeneracy commits a crime such as this, which cries to Heaven, then that individual must be looked upon no longer as a human being, but as a wild beast; and such a one, as the defendant, himself cleverly has shown, with the intention of tricking our judgment, is the most pernicious enemy of our commonwealth, for the protection of which I and you, you judges, have been placed here. Such a wild beast, by reason of his baseness, as well as on account of the danger he is to the community, deserves that he be destroyed by death and that his tracks be obliterated from the earth!

THE PRESIDING JUDGE.

Defendant Ludovicus, what more have you to say?

THE KING.

Nothing.

THE PRESIDING JUDGE.

The witnesses are excused!——The court stands adjourned until the passing of sentence.

(*The witnesses, the judges and the Attorney-General leave the chamber.*)

THE CLERK OF THE COURT.

(*Beating his head, to Alma, who sits bathed in tears over the minutes.*) Help me, holy Mary, Mother of God! The booby, with his foolishness, has blubbered all over the minutes! Not a letter can be read! The leaves are all stuck together!

ALMA.

(*Sobbing.*) O my God, he is innocent! I know that he is innocent!

THE CLERK OF THE COURT.

Why should it worry you whether he is innocent or guilty? Is it your head or his head they are going to cut off?

THE KING.

(*Who stands alone in the middle of the room, aside, but with emphasis.*) My words were, "And so at last the king's head shall fall under the headsman's axe in the market place of Perugia!"

THE CLERK OF THE COURT.

There, you see how innocent he is!

ALMA.

(*Who has risen and prays earnestly, with hands folded across her breast.*) Lord God in Heaven, Thou who hast compassion upon all the poor and miserable, preserve us from this!

THE CLERK OF THE COURT.

See now, you are a brave lad and have your heart in the right place! I shall certainly not bring you again soon to a sitting of the court. You must rewrite the whole minutes from memory at home. You will learn more from that than if you studied through the whole *corpus juris*!

THE ADVOCATE FOR THE DEFENSE.

(*Who, after the judges have left the chamber, has taken a package of bread and butter, a flask and a glass from his robe. Re places the flask and glass in front of him, and then comes forward, busy with his breakfast.*) Now, Gigi, wasn't that a Ciceronian defence that I made for you? But what do you know about Cicero! You will allow me to breakfast, of course. At first, I had the intention of sprinkling my defence with a little *curiculum vitæ*, a moving description of your cattle tending, etc. But, to be frank, Gigi, I don't believe that either would have helped you much with those (*pointing*) dunderheads out there!

THE KING.

You have my thanks for your pains, worthy Doctor Ezzelino.

(*The judges return from the council-chamber and resume their places.*)

THE PRESIDING JUDGE.

(*Reading from his notes.*) The defendant, Ludovicus, recently a tailor's apprentice in Perugia, and formerly employed in the tending of cattle in the village of Baschi, is accused of the crime of blasphemy against the holy person of the king, and is found guilty of this crime upon the evidence of unanimous testimony, as well as by his own admission. In consideration of his previous good character, as well as in consideration of his free confession, the defendant is sentenced to two years' incarceration——

ALMA.

(*Gives a muffled cry.*)

THE CLERK OF THE COURT.

Young fellow, will you hold your tongue while the judge is speaking!

THE PRESIDING JUDGE.

———and, furthermore, to ten years' deprivation of all the rights and honors of citizenship, as well as to banishment from the city of Perugia for the whole term of his life, under pain of death in case of his return.

THE CLERK OF THE COURT.

(*To Alma.*) Write, my lad! Write! This is the most important of all!

THE PRESIDING JUDGE.

(*Continuing his reading.*) In view of the important fact that the defendant has not shown the least trace of regret for his deed, the sentence provides that he shall spend his two years' incarceration in the most rigid solitary confinement.———Given in the name of the king, on the third day of the month of August, in the year of our Lord one thousand four hundred and ninety-nine. (*Turning to the guards.*) Take away the prisoner! (*Rising. To the court.*) I hereby declare to-day's session closed.

ACT III

Scene One.

A PRISON.

(*To the left, the cell door. To the right, a barred window. At the back, a folding bench, fastened against the wall.*)

THE KING.

(*Sings to a lute.*)

With an ivy wreath my brow was dressed,
In my locks there sparkled the dew;
A pair of falcons above my crest
Wove circles in the blue.

From the balcony, in joyous vein,
My mother beckoned and smiled;
At e'en thy father will come again,
In victor's garb, my child.

(*He leans the lute against the wall, sinks down upon a stool at the back of the cell and plaits a straw mat.*)——I am thirsty.——Is it really so late in the day?—— How time passes here! (*He rises and looks curiously upward through the window.*) By the Lord, the sun is beginning to glide along the south wall of the tower!——Time for the water jug! (*He fetches an earthen jug from the corner and stands expectantly before the door.*)——He will soon come!——Did I ever enjoy a drink while I was king as I do the fresh draught of water which I have received daily at this hour for the last twelfthmonth? I believe it's a stroke of good fortune that I was never in jail during my own reign.

(*The door opens noisily and a rough voice outside calls, "Water jug!" The King hastily sets the jug outside the door and returns inside the cell. The door slams shut, but is reopened immediately and the jailer enters.*)

THE JAILER.

Zounds and death, Gigi, how did you smash the jug? Silence, you dog! There's a hole in the jug. It was sound yesterday. I'll pitch into you so that your face will bleed! You take me for your servant because lately I haven't watched you so closely. You'll get it now so that your hair will turn white! Show your work!

(The King produces the unfinished straw mat.)

THE JAILER.

That your day's work! You won't get a bit of bread until you finish five times that amount! (Throwing the mat down at his feet.) There!——Now I'll inspect your cell. Look out for yourself! I won't let you out of this hole alive!

(Putting his hands behind him, he goes step by step along the wall from door to window, examining it from top to bottom, and turning around now and then at the prisoner, who stands motionless in the middle of the cell.) What does that spider web mean up there? The fourth disciplinary punishment for eight days! *(Turning around.)* You still know the seven disciplinary punishments by heart?——Hey, Gigi?

THE KING.

I know them by heart.

THE JAILER.

First disciplinary punishment?

THE KING.

Deprivation of privileges.

THE JAILER.

I'll smash that lute of yours to bits; you fritter away your working hours with it!——Second disciplinary punishment?

THE KING.

Deprivation of work.

THE JAILER.

Then see how you will spend your time! In eight days you won't be able to stand on your legs!——Third disciplinary punishment?

THE KING.

Deprivation of a soft bed at nights.——My bed is as hard as if it were stuffed with pebbles!

THE JAILER.

Silence! This rascal would like to sleep in the hay. ——Fourth disciplinary punishment?

THE KING.

Reduction of rations.

THE JAILER.

Bread and water from to-day for eight days!——Do your hear?!——Fifth disciplinary punishment?

THE KING.

Imprisonment in darkness.

THE JAILER.

Sixth disciplinary punishment?

THE KING.

Imprisonment in fetters.

THE JAILER.

By that you must understand you are chained all awry, so that after the first hour all the devils you have in your body say good-bye to you! Seventh disciplinary punishment?

THE KING.

Flogging.

THE JAILER.

(*Having reached the window.*) You shall shed your hide here yet! You, you thief, shall clamber up and down the Jacob's ladder until you fall dead. (*He passes in front of the King, leaves the cell and shuts the door from the outside.*)

THE KING.

(*Looks after him in surprise. Then quite calmly, with quiet deliberation, he turns toward the door.*) What does it mean? Where have I made a mistake? For a whole year I believed that in the course of a year I had educated this beast into a human being. Suddenly, after all that trouble, he drops back again into the animal kingdom.——Or did I dream?——It is impossible entirely that the jug should have been broken. I drank out of it this morning. He will break it now outside and then show me the pieces. Will he let me go thirsty today? Will he let me thirst?——I fear worse!——At any rate I shall receive him with a look that will make his eyes sink to the ground. (*Bracing himself.*) Help me, kingly majesty, in order that the fellow may realize his baseness of his own accord!——(*Listening.*) He's coming!——A duel without weapons, man against man!

(*The door opens noisily. Princess Alma enters, clad as in the preceding act and carrying a jug with both her hands. The door closes loudly behind her.*)

THE KING.

(*With the fright of immoderate joy.*) Alma?! My child!——Oh, beastly spite!

ALMA.

O Father, I cannot embrace you now! I bring you this jug of wine.

THE KING.

(*Struggling for breath, with both hands at his breast.*) Oh, satanic cruelty!—— (*Takes the jug from her and sets it to one side.*) Whence come you, my child? For twelve months I've thirsted for a sight of you! You are living yet, you are whole and well. Speak, how is it with you among miserable mankind?

ALMA.

We have only a few minutes! At last I have been able to bribe the jailer, and from now on he will let me visit you once a week. Tell me quickly how I can lighten your sufferings.

THE KING.

My sufferings?——Yes! What a father I am to throw my child unprotected upon the world! That is my sorrow!——Otherwise, I thank God daily that He has separated me from mankind by these six-foot walls, so that I am safe from them!

ALMA.

You can see from my appearance, Father, how good people are to me. I am still in the service of the notary. Only tell me what I may bring you to strengthen you! What frightful torments you must have endured here!

THE KING.

No, no, my child! Do not bring me anything unfamiliar into this solitude! You don't know how time passes here with the speed of the wind. In the beginning I scratched seven hundred and thirty marks on that wall, to have the daily joy of rubbing one of them out. But soon I had to blot them out by the week or by the month. And now I see with dread how quickly they grow less and less, so that the last will soon be gone and I will have to seek refuge once more under overhanging rocks and contend with wolves for their booty!——But do not let my words sadden you! You cannot guess how the jailer prepared me for your coming!

ALMA.

I think with silent horror of how fiendishly he will torment you!

THE KING.

How you imagine things! To do that he would have to be more than the weak earthworm he is. No cruelty can keep pace with my callousness. Do you know, he has shed tears of compassion here without having heard the least complaint from me! Who could so degenerate as not to be thankful when his better self finds unexpected recognition!——He could not help begrudging me the joy of seeing you again, my child. But the cowardly anxiety which springs from his calling is responsible for that. The poor man is so jealous of the ridiculous little authority vested in him by his bunch of keys that the kindness he has shown me to-day makes him afraid of becoming entirely superfluous. But didn't you suffer need in order to buy the good will of this rascal?

ALMA.

Speak not of me, Father. Time is passing and I don't know how I can help you!

THE KING.

Really, I don't know either! Were I an abler man, my fate might perhaps seem more pitiable to me. Poor as I am, I only tremble at the moment when those iron doors shall protect me no longer, when those barred windows shall prevent them reaching me, when I shall stand again among people with whom I have no mutual understanding and from whose activities I am excluded more than ever by the sentence of the law.——If you only knew how painlessly this solitude heals the gaping wounds of the soul. The judge thought he was adding to my punishment when he sentenced me to solitary confinement. How deeply I have thanked him that I do not have to live here in association with other men!

ALMA.

(*Bursting into tears.*) Lord God in Heaven! Then you don't want to see me here again!

THE KING.

(*Caressingly.*) I repay your sacrifice with discontent and ill humor. Thoughts become heavy and sluggish when a man continues talking to himself day in and day out.——Only this I ask of you; when freedom is restored to me, leave me to my fate—not forever, only until I show myself worthy of your greatness of soul.

ALMA.

Oh nevermore! Do not ask me ever to leave you! It is impossible that the future should be as bad as the past!

THE KING.

Not for you. I believe that gladly.

ALMA.

Melancholy has mastered you in this gloom. Your proud heart is almost ready to break. Nothing can be read in your face of the quiet peace you pretend to feel.

THE KING.

I have not seen my face for a year, but I can imagine how ugly it has grown. How my looks must wound your feelings!

ALMA.

Oh, do not talk like that, father!

THE KING.

But you know my imperturbable nature. And now you come in, the only thing to make my happiness complete. It is only to reward you richly and splendidly that I would become a king again.

ALMA.

I hear the jailer! Tell me how I can lighten your sufferings!

THE KING.

(*Sinks down on the stool exhausted, half to himself.*) What do I lack? How frightful this prison would become if the pleasures of life were admitted here! How can I desire here a beautiful woman, where I cannot even conjure up a recollection of beauty! My couch there is shut during the day. There is no other resting-place, and I lie down there at night as weary as if I had ploughed an acre. And in the morning the clanging bell wakes me from dreams more serene than those I dreamed as a child. (*As the door is opened.*) When you see me again, my child, you will hear no more complaints. You shall feel as happy with me as if you were outside in your sunny world. Farewell!

ALMA.

Farewell, Father! (*She leaves the cell. The door clangs behind her.*)

THE KING.

A whole long year yet!——(*He goes toward the wall.*) I will just count the marks again and see how many remain to be rubbed out.

Scene Two.

NIGHT. A WASTE.

(*Enter the King, Princess Alma, with her father's lute on her back, and a circus rider.*)

THE KING.

Have we much further to go, brother, before we come to the place where the beggars' fair is to be held?

THE CIRCUS RIDER.

We shall be there by midnight, at the latest. The real fair does not begin until then. This must be the first time you have made this pilgrimage to the gallows?

THE KING.

It is only a few moons since we joined the strollers, but, nevertheless, we have danced at many a witches' sabbath.

THE CIRCUS RIDER.

It seems to me, brother, somewhere you have unlearned marching. Otherwise you are a robust enough fellow.

THE KING.

(*Sitting down on a boulder.*) My heart beats against my ribs like a caged bird of prey. The road leads up-hill, that takes my breath!

THE CIRCUS RIDER.

We have plenty of time.——Your boy, brother, is very much better on his legs. It's a pity about him! With me he could learn something more profitable than singing street ballads to the lute. Everywhere, that's considered not much better than begging. Let him go with me, brother, if only for half a year! At any rate, it would not be worse for him than following in your footsteps, and I'll make a rider out of him after whom the circus managers will break their necks!

THE KING.

Don't take me for an ass, dear brother; how can you make my boy succeed as a circus rider when you yourself must trudge afoot!

THE CIRCUS RIDER.

You are as suspicious as if you had kegs full of gold at home, while from all appearances you don't remember when you had warm food last! You won't get anywhere that, way! To-night at the beggars' fair we shall meet at least half a dozen circus managers. They gather there to look for artists to appear with them. Then you will see, you poor devil, how they will contend for me and how one will outbid the other! Thank God, I am not so unknown as you, you gutter singers! And if I get my job again, I shall have horses enough for your merry boy to break his neck the first day, if he has the mind!

THE KING.

Tell me, brother, does one find theatre managers too at the beggars' fair?

THE CIRCUS RIDER.

Theatre managers too, certainly. The theatre managers come there from all over the country. Where else would they get their dancers and their clowns! Frankly, brother, it seems very doubtful to me your getting an engagement. You don't look as if you could act a farce.

THE KING.

But there is a higher art, called tragedy!

THE CIRCUS RIDER.

Tragedy, yes, I have heard that name!——I understand nothing about that art, dear brother. I only know that it is miserable poor pay.——(*To Alma.*) Now, my brave lad, doesn't your mouth water for better fodder?——Do you want to learn circus riding with me?

THE KING.

(*Getting up.*) Forward, brother, do not let us miss the beggars' fair. Fortune only offers us her hand once a year!

(*Exeunt.*)

Scene Three.

(Night. The gallows looms in the background. Forward, to the left, is a gigantic boulder, beneath a gnarled oak, which serves the performers as a stage. In front of it flickers a huge bonfire, about which are gathered the spectators, men, women and children, in fantastic raiment.)

(Chorus)

Both in town and country beds,
With their windows tightly fastened, honest folk are
drowsing.
Those with no home for their heads
Dance with merry spectres 'neath the gallows tree carousing.
Exiles from the sun's bright light,
Fortune's tracks we still can follow in the dark obscurely,
And are lords in our own sight
While in heaven the friendly stars twinkle quite demurely.

A THEATRE MANAGER.

(In a bass voice to an actor.) Show me what you have learned, my worthy young friend. *Hic Rhodus hic salta!* What is your act?

THE ACTOR.

I act the fool, honored master.

THE THEATRE MANAGER.

Then act the fool, young friend, but act him well! Difficile est satiram non scribere! My public is used only to the best!

THE ACTOR.

I will give you a sample of my art at once.

THE THEATRE MANAGER.

If you find favor in my eyes, young friend, you shall have a hundred soldi a month. *Pacta exacta——boni amici*! Go, young friend, and give your proof.

(*The Actor mounts the rock. He is received with hand-clapping and cries of "bravo" by the spectators.*)

THE ACTOR.

(*Breaks first into laughter, then speaks the following lines, accompanying each couplet with a different kind of titter.*)

Count Onofrio was a man
As stupid as a ram,
And he had daughters seven
He wanted paired up even.
Their way no suitor bent his legs.
Rotten eggs! Rotten eggs!

THE AUDITORS.

(*Have interrupted this effort several times with hisses and whistles. At the last words they pelt the actor with clumps of earth, while with shrill whistling they repeat the words.*)
Rotten eggs! Rotten eggs!

THE THEATRE MANAGER.

(*Blaring out above the rest of the noise.*) Down with the rascal! A page! The Lord God created him in wrath! *Alea est jacta*!

(*The Actor leaves the rock.*)

(*Chorus.*)

Nor believe not, human brood,
That pursuit of idle dreams fills our whole existence;
Lovers' ways are somewhat crude
When the night wind dead men's bones rattles with persistence!

(*The King, Princess Alma and a Procuress appear on the scene.*)

THE PROCURESS.

Now, ballad singer, how much will you take for that pretty boy of yours?—
—Listen to the pleasant clang of the goldpieces in my pocket!

THE KING.

Just now a circus rider wanted to buy him from me. Leave me and my boy in peace! I didn't come to the beggars' fair for this. Besides, what can you want with my boy!

THE PROCURESS.

Don't think I am so stupid, ballad singer, that I can't see that your boy is a girl! The sweet child will find a mother in me, more full of love for her than any one in the wide, wide world. (*To Alma.*) Don't tremble so, my pretty little dove! I won't eat you! When one grows up with such a pretty figure and such a round, rosy face, with fresh cherry lips and dark glowing eyes, one sleeps beneath silken covers and not in the open fields. You will not have to play the lute with me. Only to be charming. What pleasanter life can sprightly young blood desire? You will meet ministers of state and barons at my house; you will only have to chose. Have you ever been kissed by a real baron? That tastes better than a tramp's unshaven face!——Look here, ballad singer! Here are two undipped ducats. The girl belongs to me! It's a bargain!

THE KING.

Go snick up, you and your gold!——(*To Alma.*) That fool woman, in her stupidity, really takes you for a girl in boy's clothes! Why aren't you? If you were a girl, there would be no better opportunity than this to rid yourself of the bristly ballad singer! There is nothing worse than passing 'round the hat for pennies. Perhaps you have already gathered pennies thrown you by the compassionate foster-daughters of this worthy dame?! They always have a chance of being forced again into the exalted ranks of burghers' society as worthy members. Our star is not in the ascendant.

THE PROCURESS.

(*To Alma.*) Don't allow this vagabond to set your head whirling, for Heaven's sake, my dear! You don't know how cozy my house is! The whole day you can amuse yourself with a band of the liveliest companions. If the ballad singer won't sell you to me, let's run away from him. Don't be afraid of him! You will be as safe under my protection as if you were surrounded by a whole army corps.

ALMA.

(*Wrenching herself from the Procuress grasp.*) I will speak to him. (*Goes from her to the King. With trembling voice.*) Do you remember, my father, why we came to this beggars' fair?

THE KING.

I know, my child. (*He mounts the rock and is received until dry coughs. Then he speaks in a clear tone, but with inward emotion.*)

I am the ruler over all this land,
By God anointed, but by no one known!
And should I shriek until the mountains bent
That I am ruler over all this land,
The very birds would chirp a mock at me!
What profit then is this, my kingly thought
When hungering I snap with eager teeth,
As in the winter months the starving beasts?
But not to make a plaint of all my woes
Come I, my folk, to you!

THE SPECTATORS.

(*Break into shrill laughter, applaud stormily and cry loudly.*) Da capo! Da capo!

THE KING.

(*Anxiously and with embarrassment.*) Kind audience! My specialty on the stage is great and serious tragedy!

THE SPECTATORS.

(*Laughing loudly.*) Bravo! Bravo!

THE KING.

(*With all the force of his soul.*) What I have just told you is to me the dearest, the holiest thing that I have kept in the depths of my soul until now!

THE SPECTATORS.

(*Give vent to a new storm of approval, from out of which the words can be plainly heard.*) A remarkable comedian! An unusual character actor!

THE THEATRE MANAGER.

(*Who has mounted a rock back of the crowd in order to hear better.*) Finish your monologue, my dear young friend! Or does your poor brain harbor only these few crumbs?——*Si tacuisses, philosophus mansisses!*

THE KING.

Very well, then! But I ask you from my heart, kind audience, to give my words the earnest meaning which belongs to them! How shall I succeed in moving your hearts, if you do not believe the plaints which come from my mouth!

THE SPECTATORS.

(*Laugh and applaud enthusiastically.*) What a pose he assumes!——And such droll grimaces!——Go on with your farce!

THE THEATRE MANAGER.

(*Hissing.*) Children! Children! Nothing is worse for the actor than applause! If you succeed in making him overvalue himself, the poor rogue will be capable only of the lowest kind of trash! *Odi profanum vulgus et arceo!* (*To the King.*) Continue, my son! It seems to me as if your parodies might amuse my enlightened public!

THE KING.

(*Seeking by every means to invest his speech with earnestness.*)

I am the ruler! To your knees with you!
What mean these bursts of mad, indecent mirth!
'Tis my own fault that here, in this my realm,
None knows me more. My sentinels slumber,
My doughty warriors serve another's wage.
I lack that highest earthly might, the gold!
Still, ever yet, was there a rightful king
Who spent his time in counting out his coin?
That task he graciously accords to slaves!
The farthing, soiled with sweat of tradesmen's toil
Was never struck with an intent to smirch
The hands of those anointed of the Lord!

THE SPECTATORS.

(*Breaking out into the wildest laughter.*) Da capo! ——Bravo!——Da capo!

A THEATRE MANAGER.

This man is a brilliant satirist! A second Juvenal!

THE KING.

(*As before.*)

I am the ruler!——He of you who doubts
Let him stand forth!——I'll prove my claim to him!
I was not wont before to praise myself,

But now the world has robbed me of that pride.
To him who wears a dagger at his hip
I'll teach the art of sinking it with grace
Into his foeman's breast; so that the duel,
From a rude spectacle of sweat and blood,
Becomes as pleasant as an el fen dance
And even death puts on a sweeter garb!——
I am the ruler!——From the herd of barbs
Bring me the wildest of unbroken steeds;
Nor trouble you with saddle nor with bit;
Let him but feel my heels press in his flanks
He'll pant beneath me in the Spanish gait
And from that time be tractable to ride.
I am the ruler! Come unto the feast!
The world is distant with its petty ills,
The evening star illuminates our meal,
From distant arcades mellow songs arise.
The guest may wander through the twilight green
Where, from the shelter of a plashing fall,
The sportive nymphs will lure him with their wiles.
I am the king! Go fetch a maiden here!
Let her be chaste as is the morning dew!
I'll not awake her innocent alarms;
I come a beggar with an empty scrip;
Six steps away from her I'll stand. Warn her
'Gainst wiles of Satan! 'Ere a star grows pale
I'll move, not only body, but her son!
Bring me the truest wife among them all!
She soon shall doubt if loathing or if faith
Is greater pander to the lusts of flesh
And, doubtingly, shall offer me her lips.
I am the king! What child is here as small
In hands and feet, or even in his joints!
With scorn I look upon you as you laugh,
Your feet may jig, your hands may fan the air,
The brains within your skulls are very stale!
So be it!——Will the slimmest maiden here
Venture to dance with me in trial of skill?
She never knew the bloody task of war
And all her joints are quite as small as mine.

(*As nobody offers, to Alma.*) Reach me a torch, my child!

(*Alma takes a glowing brand from the bonfire and hands it to the King. Then, standing at the foot of the rock, she plays a melody on her lute.*)

(*The King gracefully and with dignity dances a few steps of a courtly torch dance, then throws the glowing brand back into the fire.*)

(*The Spectators give vent to prolonged applause.*)

THE ACTOR.

(*Rising from amid the spectators, in a tone of parody.*)

I am the monarch over all this land——

THE SPECTATORS.

Down with the barber's assistant. He has no appreciation! Strike him to earth!

THE THEATRE MANAGER.

Quod licet Jovi, non licet bovi!——(*To the King, who has left the rock.*) I will engage you as ballet master and character actor and offer you a hundred soldi a month.

ANOTHER THEATRE MANAGER.

(*Speaking in a falsetto voice.*) Hundred soldi, hi, hi, hi? A hundred soldi will the skinflint give you?——I wave a hundred and fifty in your face, you rascal! What do you say, hi, hi, hi?——Will you now or won't you?

THE KING.

(*To the First Theatre Manager.*) Don't you think, honored master, that I am rather a tragedian than a comedian?

THE FIRST THEATRE MANAGER.

You haven't the least trace of talent as a tragedian; as character actor, on the contrary, there is no chance of it going ill with you again in this world. Believe me, my dear friend, I know these kings. I have eaten dinner with two of them at once! Your king's monologue is the caricature of a real king and will be valued as such.

THE SECOND THEATRE MANAGER.

Don't let yourself be hoodwinked by this horse dealer, you rascal! What does he know about comedy! I have studied my profession at the universities of Rome and Bologna. How about two hundred soldi, hi, hi, hi?

THE FIRST THEATRE MANAGER.

(*Clapping the King on the shoulder.*) I'll give you three hundred soldi, my dear young friend!

THE SECOND THEATRE MANAGER.

I'll give you four hundred soldi, you dirty rogue, hi, hi, hi!

THE FIRST THEATRE MANAGER.

(*Giving the King his purse.*) Here is my purse! Put it in your pocket and keep it as a souvenir of me!

THE KING.

(*Pocketing the purse.*) Will you engage my boy, too?

THE FIRST THEATRE MANAGER.

Your boy? What has he learned?

ALMA.

I play Punchinello, honored master.

THE FIRST THEATRE MANAGER.

Let me see him at once, your Punchinello.

ALMA.

(*Mounts the rock and speaks in fresh, lively tones.*)

Fortune's pranks are so astounding
That her whims none can foresee;
Sure, I find them so confounding
Smiles nor tears come not to me.

Heaven itself is scarcely steady,
O'er our heads it's turning yet,
Mankind then had best be ready
For a daily somerset.

Mischief, when his legs can trip it
When his arms are pliant still
Is so lovable a snippet
That he's sure of your good will!

THE SPECTATORS.

(*Show their approval.*)

THE FIRST THEATRE MANAGER.

I'll engage this puppy as the youngest Punchinello in the business.——We will wander to-night *per pedes Apostulorum* to Siena, where my company presents tragedy, farce and tragic-comedy. From thence to Modena, to Perugia——

THE KING.

Before we reach Perugia, I shall have to break my contract. I am banished that city under pain of death.

THE FIRST THEATRE MANAGER.

Under what name did that happen to you, my young friend?

THE KING.

I am called Ludovicus.

THE FIRST THEATRE MANAGER.

I name you Epaminondas Alexandrion! That was the name of a wonderfully talented comedian who eloped with my wife a short time ago. *Nomen est omen!*——Come, my children. (*Leaves with the King and Alma.*)

CHORUS.

Soon the sun will rise in state,
Us to scatter for a year; here and there upon the wind,
Driven by relentless Fate,
To hunt illusive phantoms none of us can ever find.

ACT IV

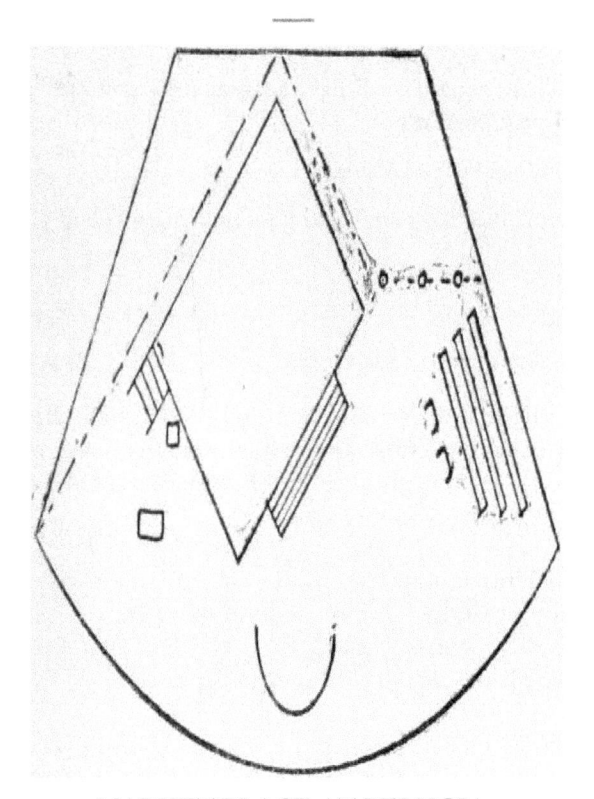

MARKET PLACE AT PERUGIA.

(In the midst of the market place is a simple stage, from which a flight of steps leads to the spectators' seats, as shown in the above plan. A rope separates the auditorium from the rest of the market place. The back of the stage is curtained off. To the left, a small stairway leads from the stage to a space which serves as a dressing room. The King is kneeling in this space, before a little mirror, making up his face to resemble a majestic kingly mask. He is smooth shaven, is in his shirt sleeves and is clad simply, but richly. Princess Alma sits near him, on an upturned box, with her left foot over her right knee, tuning her lute. She wears a tasteful punchinello's dress, all of white, composed of tights, a close-fitting jacket, trimmed with fur, and a high pointed hat.)

THE KING.

Have you chanced to hear, my child, how the advance sale is today?

ALMA.

How can you have any doubts about that? The announcement that you were to appear sold all the seats for to-day's performance by sundown yesterday. Indeed, all Perugia knows already that your art far exceeds anything they saw in Epaminondas Alexandrion hitherto.

THE KING.

At the bottom of my soul, I was never pained before that my laurels increased the fame of another. The assumed name protected me from too mortifying a contact with humanity. Even in my most daring dreams I cannot imagine how I would look today upon a throne. Perhaps, after all, I am fit for something higher in this world than dishing out, day by day, the recollections of vanished pomp to the childish rabble as the copy of real majesty.

ALMA.

In how happy a mood you have been wherever we have played! It even seems to me as if you found our stormy success some slight reward for all the long years of sorrow.

THE KING.

Don't listen to me any longer, my child, or you will lose your joyousness and appear before the public not as a punchinello, but as a spectre from the grave!

ALMA.

Of course, here in the market place of Perugia you must feel uncomfortable.

A PAGE.

(*Enters the dressing room carrying an autograph album under his arm.*) My mistress, the noble spouse of the honorable Doctor Silvio Andreotti, Attorney General to His Majesty the King, sends me thither. My mistress desires the celebrated artist Epaminondas Alexandrion to place his autograph in this book. My mistress bids me say that the book contains only the autographs of the greatest men. (*He hands the book and writing materials to the King.*)

THE KING.

(*Takes the goose quill and writes, speaking the words aloud as he does so.*) "Only simplicity can fathom wisdom," Epaminondas Alexandrion the Second.

(*Giving back the album.*) Present my respects to your noble mistress, the spouse of the Attorney General to the King.

(*Exit the page.*)

THE KING.

(*Making himself ready.*) Another wrinkle here, so! ——You, my treasure, indeed, appear to have found happiness in our present calling.

ALMA.

Yes, father! A thousand times, yes! My heart is full of the joy of living, since I see my acting received daily with crowded benches!

THE KING.

It astonishes me how little our environment affects you, although you allow all to believe that they are your equals by birth. You are a lamb among a pack of wolves, each of which has sworn to protect you, because each one grudges you to the others. But wolves remain wolves! And if the lamb does not want to be torn to pieces finally, it must, sooner or later, become a wolf itself.——But don't listen to me! I do not understand what evil spirit influences me today to call down misfortune upon our heads!

ALMA.

Do not believe me capable of such base ingratitude, Father, as to think that the pleasure I find in my work as a punchinello prevents me recollecting with joy the noble pomp in which I passed my childhood!

THE KING.

(*Rising with forced composure.*) At any rate, I am ready for the very worst!

(*As he speaks these words the theatre servants place two golden seats in front of the first row of benches. Immediately after, the Theatre Manager rushes into the dressing room in the greatest excitement.*)

THE THEATRE MANAGER.

Alexandrion! Brother! Let me clasp you in my arms! (*He embraces and kisses him.*) You pearl of dramatic art! Shall I make you speechless with pride!—— ——His Majesty the King is coming to the performance! His Majesty the King of Umbria and His Royal Highness the Crown Prince Filipo! Have you words?! I have had two golden chairs put in front of the first row. The moment their Highnesses seat themselves Punchinello must appear on the stage with a deep bow! So be ready, children!——And you, Alexandrion, apple of my eye, bring to light today all the richest treasures hidden in the depths of your soul! As I (*gesture*) turn this glove inside out, so do you turn your inside outside! Let our royal auditors hear things such as have not been heard in any theatre since the time of Plautus and of Terence.

THE KING.

(*Putting on his jacket.*) I was just asking myself whether it might not be better for me to present my royal visitors with something different from my king's farce; perhaps the morning dreams of the old tailor's apprentice, or those of the swineherd. The old tailor's apprentice would give our guests plenty of material for laughter and that is all they expect, while the king's farce might hurt their feelings.

THE THEATRE MANAGER.

Ha, ha! You are afraid of being locked up again for *lèse majesté*! Nonsense! Give your king's farce! Make it stronger than you have ever played it! If royalty honors us, it is because it wants to see the king's farce! What harm can they do us? *Ultra posse nemo tenetur!* Well, what did I prophesy to you when I picked you from the scum of the land there at the beggars' fair! Today we perform before crowned heads! *Per aspera ad astra!*——(*Exit.*)

(*During this scene the spectators' seats have become filled with an aristocratic public; outside the ropes the crowd gathers thickly. During the following words the King dons a royal black beard, puts on his wig, sets the golden crown on his head and throws a heavy purple mantle across his shoulders.*)

THE KING.

My head was to fall beneath the headsman's axe in this market place if ever I dared return to Perugia without foreswearing my right to the crown.—— Instead of that, how much have I had to foreswear to tread my native soil for the second time! The delight of satisfied revenge; the manly duty of preserving my inheritance for my family; all the good things of earth which fortune lavished on me in my cradle, and now even the naked dignity of human nature which forbids even the slave from offering himself as an entertainment to those condemned along with him!

ALMA.

And a thousand voices praise you as an artist the like of which never spoke to his folk before. How many king's names are forgotten!

THE KING.

I do not value that! Only a day laborer or a place hunter can wear with pride the laurels which spring from earthly misery! But do you know what pride is possible to me in this existence? Called to an inscrutable trial, I struggle here as only one of a million beings. But King Nicola, as king, met death! No one doubts but that he is long beyond the reach of human humiliation. No one asks him now to renounce the dignity conferred on him by God. No shadow disturbs his kingly remembrance! I owe it to this illusion that I am still alive under God's sun. And until the hour of my death no storm shall deprive me of this possession, which, perhaps, I can still dispose of to your advantage! My sceptre! My orb! (*He takes both from the property chest.*) And now—the—ki-ki-king's farce! (*Seized by a sudden pain in the heart, he strives painfully for breath.*)

ALMA.

(*Rushing to his side.*) Jesu, Maria, my father; I can see how marble white you are through your make-up!

THE KING.

A shortness of breath!———It is over.———I have been subject to it since I was in prison———

(*King Pietro and Prince Filipo enter the auditorium and take their places in the golden chairs.*)

THE THEATRE MANAGER.

(*Calling behind the scenes.*) On the stage, Punchinello!

THE KING.

(*Springing up.*) Go! Go! I feel entirely well!

ALMA.

(*Seizing a fool's bauble, rushes on the stage, bows, and then declaims in a light, jesting tone.*)

I here appear to herald unto you
The coming of a king, who, verily,
Was never king.———
Groom of the bedchamber is my post to him.
I laud him as a demigod, a hero;
Give admiration to his wit; praise his clothes;
My profit great in offices and gifts.
I earnestly desire him length of days;
But, should he die and his successor rule———
I trust God's grace will spare me from that blow!———
Why then, obsequiously, with raptured mien
To the newcomer I shall play my rôle,
As is a valet courtier's pious way.
But I must cease, for lo, the King is here!

THE KING.

(*Enters.*) My slumbers have been light throughout the night.

ALMA.

(*Bowing, with crossed arms.*) Tour people should be made to smart for that!

THE KING.

My people? Made to suffer? When my mind
Fears I alone should carry all the blame?
What more have I achieved than other men
That I am called to rule it o'er my kind!
Away from off the steps unto my throne!
Slumber forsook my weary eyes last night
Because I, driven by the power of law,
Signed a death warrant when the hour was late!
Avaunt, you worm! And never venture more
Your head within the limits of my wrath!

ALMA.

(*Turning to the audience.*)

You see, respected auditors, how hard
It may be candidly to make one's way!
In lack of fitting words for my defence,
My plight with resignation I accept.
Dejected is my exit through this door,
But by another I shall soon return.

(*She comes down the stairway toward the audience backward, then sits down, on the steps facing the public.*)

THE KING.

(*To himself.*)

Half my lifetime I have striven now
To make my eyes more sharp, to clear my wits,
That my dear folk might reap the benefit!

ALMA.

(*Speaking to the public.*)

Instead of that he might do something wise.
Who gives him thanks? His people whisper low,
His mind is lacking quite in brilliancy,
And his sublime example serves as jest!

THE KING.

(*With uplifted hands.*)

Illuminate me with thy light, O God,
That I depart not from thy chosen way,
That good and evil I may quickly learn!
If thy reflected splendor shine from me
The people cannot blindly mock my rule;
Nor inefficiency mislead my steps!

ALMA.

(*Springing up.*)

I can, however! (*She steps upon the stage.*)
As you see me now,
I am a woman, decked with all the charms
To fan your kingly thoughts into a blaze!
The flower of innocence remains unplucked
To gratify you with its purity.
Groaning beneath the weight of majesty,
With sublime chastity your wedded bride,
You yet may enter Pleasure's magic path.
Be ruler! Learn to blush as other men,
And do not join the devil's league with death,
In profanation of creation's work.
'Tis fit the hero and the anchorite
Should pray with deep humility to God
To sanctify and make them holy beings.
Before the Lord shall call you to himself
May not some earthly bliss be yours by right;
Do you not fear to come from Egypt Land
Without a good view of the pyramids!

THE KING.

And should I riot in luxurious ease,
Who would protect my folk? Who hear their cry?

ALMA.

That task I willingly would undertake.
Since childhood it has been my constant use
To ride a horse unbroken to the bit,
To crush his wildness in a frenzied gait.
Thy folk shall grow to know no higher law
Than to administer thy joy and gain.

THE KING.

Depart from out my house, you brazen trull,
Before I stamp a mark upon your brow
With glowing iron!

ALMA.

Once more the lightning!
My looks do not find favor in his sight!
(*Going up to the last step.*)
My honored hearers, can you tell me now
Where lies the weakness of this curious king?
Else, from his wrathful gestures, much I fear
Our farce is apt to change to tragedy!

KING PIETRO.

(*To Alma.*) You must approach him as minister, or chancellor, and inform him that it is just his wisdom which brings misery upon the land. If he listens to your words, he is nothing but a fool; if he does not listen, you can boldly call him a tyrant!

ALMA.

(*Bowing.*)

I'll do as you suggest. With all my heart
I thank you for your counsel, gracious lord!
(*She mounts the stage once more; to the King.*)
With deep dismay, I see Your Majesty's
August rule in danger. From every side
The mob comes streaming to the palace walls.
To me, your loyal chancellor, 'tis clear,
Instead of shooting down this threatening herd,
No better means can now be found to quell
Their spirit than to send them forth to fight
Against the neighboring principalities.
The mob grows weary of the golden hours
And frets against the long continued peace;
It thirsts for blood, like the wild beast it is.
Its drunken lust will crown you conqueror
Amid the corpses fallen from its ranks!
Heaven itself bestows this last respite.
Seize, then, the sword! Else, even in this hour,
Yourself may fall with many deadly wounds.

KING PIETRO.

Excellently spoken! (*Turning to the Crown Prince.*) Do you remember, my son, to what frightful expedients Bernardo Ruccellai wanted to force me when I forbade the citizens to extend the carnival a week? The pretty boy spoke as if he had been there.

(*After these words the audience gives vent to short, but energetic, applause.*)

PRINCE FILIPO.

The actors are exceptionally good. Let us hear them further, my honored father.

KING PIETRO.

I am most keen to learn what rejoinder my able spokesman will meet up there.

THE KING.

My life!——Take that!——The people's uproar frights
Me not! Before they suffer by my fault,
Why let them in their madness slaughter me!
In time to come, ensanguined with my blood,
They will become a dread unto themselves,
And, worshipful, return to Reason's shrine.
My death will serve its purpose thousand fold!
As payment for your spiteful plan of war,
I here dismiss you as my chancellor.
Be happy you have 'scaped the headsman's axe!

KING PIETRO.

Kingly words that I should like to have spoken myself! If only one could find a better chancellor so easily! (*To Alma.*) I am sorry, my young diplomat, that my advice served you so ill.

(*Another outburst of applause from the spectators.*)

ALMA.

(*Turning to the public.*)

Once more my well-laid plan has gone astray!——
Before, dear sirs, I yet proceed to show
How I can bring this hero to his knees,
So that he cries beneath my scornful lash,
And whining drags himself unto my feet,
A sorry object, broken to his soul,
Begging that I shall lift him up again
And dampening all the dust about with tears,——

Before I show my skill in this respect,
I ask you to unlace your purses' strings
And to bestow a little of your wealth
With open hands upon my humble self.

(*She takes two white plates and comes down the steps.*)

Merely a pause, respected auditors,
A little contribution's all I ask!

(*She passes among the rows of spectators, collecting from them, but does not approach the royal entourage. The King wanders about the stage speaking a monologue.*)

THE KING.

Conflict on conflict! Should my strength be spent,
Death, like a living flame, would rush unchecked
Throughout the confines of the realm!

(*To the public.*)

An obolus will serve, most honored sirs!

ALMA.

(*To a spectator who puts his arm about her waist and attempts to kiss her.*)

Oh, fie, good sir, you scarcely are polite!
Besides, I'm not a girl; pray keep your place!

THE SPECTATOR.

I never yet saw boyish hand so slim!

THE KING.

(*To the public.*)

An obolus is quite enough, good sirs!

(*To himself.*)

Would it were over!——Beyond betterment;
I yet await what store of future ills
Malicious fortune still may deal to me!

(*To the public.*)

Only an obolus, good sirs, I ask!

(*King Pietro beckons Alma to him and lays a gold piece upon her plate.*)

THE KING.

(*Bowing his thanks to the audience.*)

What is more happy than the artist's soul!
Misfortune is a spring of joy to him;
He shapes a pleasure from a wild lament.
Adversity indeed, may clip his wings,
But at the sound of gold he soon recalls
His inborn kinship to humanity.

(*Alma returns to the stage and' empties the plates into the King's hand. He estimates the sum quickly, thrusts the money into his purple mantle, then, turning to his daughter, continues.*)

THE KING.

Once more, deceptive shape, you dare to tread
Before my eyes. Who are you? Let me know!

ALMA.

I am yourself!

THE KING.

Myself! But I am that!

ALMA.

Which of us two is right will soon appear!
Before you, mangled by a beast of prey,
There lies a corpse. The blame belongs to you!

THE KING.

I murdered him! How know you of such things?

ALMA.

And do you see the stakes all round about?

THE KING.

That, too, is known to you?

ALMA.

'Tis living flesh,
Encased in tow and tar!

THE KING.

His cry of pain
Was music to my ear! It cost me much!

ALMA.

The living entrails on the altar red,
Even today are used by you to move
The innocent to choice of peace or war!

THE KING.

How came you by such store of frightful facts?
In deep repentance now I tear my hair!
My royal might seductive proved!

ALMA.

A jest,
You're clasping at your quickly beating heart,
The while your eyes still shadow forth their greed!

THE KING.

'Tis not a jest!

ALMA.

It is!

THE KING.

Nevertheless,
Spare me worse!

ALMA.

Childish bodies, glowing pure,
Are made a sacrifice unto your lust,
That you may see their tender limbs contort.

THE KING.

No! Nevermore!

ALMA.

You see, you must give way.
That shows that you are weak and I am strong!

THE KING.

(*Sinking to his knees.*)

Have mercy!

ALMA.

Have you ever yet
Obtained victory in strife with me?

THE KING.

(*Weeping.*)

Behold my head is bent unto the earth
By pains of hell!

ALMA.

Then pluck up heart again,
Torture of innocents will calm your own!

THE KING.

(*With trembling voice.*)

You beast, you are the stronger of us twain,
But grant a brief respite before I heap
New cruelties upon forgotten ones.
I crawl like any worm upon the dust.
My better self, which I have lost to you,
Begs that you do not press your might too far.
New victims soon will fall within my clutch;
The tongue which has already tasted blood
Beseeches you to save them from its rage.

KING PIETRO.

(*Rising from his chair.*) You carry your jests somewhat too far up there! What will the foolish multitude think when it sees royal majesty so brought to dust!

ALMA.

(*To the public.*)

Folly can show the naked truth beneath
The glittering facts on history's page.

(*To the King.*)

I'll spare you, then.—But first take solemn oath
To cherish good always within your heart!

THE KING.

I swear!

(*Looking up in tears.*)

You ask me that!——I'm in a maze!
Who are you?

ALMA.

I am your dream! Your dæmon!
Awake to higher efforts from my ban,
I call on you to rise above yourself!

THE KING.

(*Rises and runs anxiously up and down.*)

And if Methuselah I should outlive
That frightful error I shall ne'er forget!
Under the cover of the shamed night
The torch flares out: Blazing in wild array,
Consuming flames run through the heated limbs;
Vice sings its victory; lecherous hell
Is jubilant; the rising flood of crime
O'erflows its banks; and deeds the gray-haired wastrel,
Tortured by flames of lust, could not achieve,
Stagger in kinship to the drunken thought!
——Oh, take my praise, thou golden light of day!

ALMA.

(*To the public.*)

With this I make an ending to our play.
Your pardon, if its setting troubled you.
My sole desire was merely to exploit
That ancient, well-liked acrobatic trick (gesture)
By which a man climbs up on his own head.

KING PIETRO.

(*To the King.*) And you call that a farce, my dear friend?! See, you have brought the tears to my eyes!

THE KING.

(*After he has laid aside the crown.*) Will your Majesty believe it, our piece has been received everywhere as a harmless farce?

KING PIETRO.

I cannot believe that! Are my subjects so stupid? Otherwise, how can you explain it to me?

THE KING.

I cannot inform your Majesty as to that. Such is life!

KING PIETRO.

Very well, then, if such is life, my people shall not hear you again, until they understand you, for otherwise your play would only undermine the power of my throne. Lay aside your mantle and stand forth before me!

(*The King lays aside mantle, beard and wig and descends the steps.*)

KING PIETRO.

I cannot appoint a man who has made his living collecting pennies to any office of state. But my royalty shall never prevent me from making a companion of the man whose gifts have moved me to tears. There is a post vacant close to the throne, which I have left unfilled until now, because I did not wish to make a place for folly in a position where even the greatest amount of wisdom is too small. But you shall fill this position. You shall be powerless against the meanest citizen of my state. But your high mental power shall stand between me and my people, between me and the royal chancellors; it shall be allowed to expend itself unpunished upon me and my son. As there on the stage, your soul stood between the ruler and his dark desires, so shall it check my innermost self! I appoint you my court fool! ——Follow me! (*He starts to go.*)

THE THEATRE MANAGER.

(*Wringing his hands and with tears in his eyes, throws himself on his knees before King Pietro.*) *Moriturus te salutat!* Your gracious Majesty's unworthy theatre manager, who single-handed plucked this exceptional tragedian from the gallows, now has his life blighted by your Majesty's gracious choice!

KING PIETRO.

We bestow upon you the privilege of giving performances untaxed for twenty years!

THE KING.

May I inform your Majesty that I am the father of this young girl and that the father will appreciate your goodness even more than the actor if he may hope that his child will no longer need to conceal her true nature.

KING PIETRO.

Was I so deceived! (*To Alma.*) I do not want to hear your audacious speeches again from a woman's mouth. (*To the King.*) Let your child follow you! (*He leaves the theatre in company with the Prince.*)

ACT V

THE THRONE ROOM.

(The King in court costume. His office of court fool is shown discreetly by a suitable head covering. In his languid hand he holds a short bauble. He appears strangely altered: his pale face is deeply lined and his eyes seem twice as large as formerly.)

THE KING.

How strange is life! During many years of hardship of every description I felt my bodily strength increase daily. Each sunrise found me brighter in spirits, stronger in muscle. No mishap caused me to doubt the sturdiness of my constitution. And since I have been living here in peace and plenty I am shriveling like an apple in springtime. I feel life going from me step by step and the doctors agree in shrugging their shoulders and saying with long faces that they cannot foresee the outcome.——Did I ever reign in these halls? Every day since I came here I have asked myself the same question, and every day it seems more nonsensical. It is as hard for me to believe as it would be for me to credit anyone who told me that I had lived on another planet. King Pietro is the worthiest prince who ever had a throne, and I am the last person in his realm who would want to change places with him. That is my last word each evening, a word which does not make me dream of the thick prison air, but of the dripping, stormbent, rustling trees, of the gloomy heaths, of the virgin dew on the thick grass, of my journeys from place to place on the stroller's vans, on the tailboards of which I made all hearts waver between pity and respect.——I have noticed an unusual cramp in my left arm for the last few days. It is not gout, it is not the weakness of old age. But before my failing members give way, I have a work to accomplish. Let me complete it, O Fate, so that we may part in friendship! I have cultivated it with all possible care, as the only thing profitable in my life. Or shall I be the dupe again? Perhaps, the eager young hearts really do not need my help? Does egotism make me overestimate by importance in furthering their union? Who will open my eyes to my true merits? Blind I came, must I go so? I go and listen! Later I shall not have to think about the answers. (*Exit.*)

(Enter King Pietro and Crown Prince Filipo.)

KING PIETRO.

I have made inquiries among the Medici in Florence if they are willing that a daughter of their house should become your wife. I have just received word that the Medici, confident in the permanency of our rule, would welcome such an alliance.

FILIPO.

Before you did that, my respected father, I had distinctly told you that I shall never marry any one but Donna Alma, Alexandrion's daughter!

KING PIETRO.

(*In anger.*) The daughter of my court fool! You belong back in the shop whence you came!

FILIPO.

Then send me back to the shop, respected father!

KING PIETRO.

Although there can be no doubt of this maiden's virtues, the general welfare of the state demands that you wed a prince's daughter. If you desired to court the daughter of a citizen of Perugia, I might be able to countenance your mesalliance without slapping our own origin in the face. Even then, your choice would be an offense against the state, which would result in party strife and violence among the citizens. But if you chose a queen of obscurist origin for your people, then you show at once that you undervalue the duties of a prince. Who can tell what heirs may spring from such a marriage! Instead of looking forward to your reign with confidence, they will await it with sullen dread, anxiety and insubordination. Did I overcome King Nicola and drive him to an early death that my son should indulge in madness such as cost that monarch his life and throne?! That is the reason I brought Alexandrion here, because he has meditated upon just such serious questions! (*Lifting a portière.*) Call the fool! Now he shall show me if his wisdom can withstand the call of blood! Now he shall show me if he can follow his own sermons as I do, or if he is only an empty chatterer!

THE KING.

(*Entering.*) What does my dear lord desire?

KING PIETRO.

I have been beholden to you for advice in the hours of the most frightful danger. Had I not followed freely your advice, so full of watchful and crafty shrewdness, in difficult situations we might today be under foreign rule. Now, however, I require of you a sacrifice which, as the father of your child, you owe the state and our dynasty. Without restraint I allowed your intelligence to rule between me and my own blood, never suspecting how soon I should have to ask you to put it between yourself and your child. The Prince asks me to give him your daughter for his wife!

THE KING.

My child is so far above me that her feet never touch the ground without the seed of happiness blossoming beneath her tread.

KING PIETRO.

I can believe that, but will you order your daughter to reject every offer of the Prince!

FILIPO.

Donna Alma will never obey that order!

KING PIETRO.

Silence!

THE KING.

I can order nothing in this country.

KING PIETRO.

That is true! But you must obey!

THE KING.

That is true! But my daughter need not obey!

KING PIETRO.

Enough of your jests! I am sorry I overprized your wisdom. You understand that your refusal ends your stay here at my court. I am pained to see your calm deliberation forsake you at this pass. You are a bad father, Alexandrion, in not fearing to deprive your child of my good will! In order to protect myself against the reproach of ingratitude, I shall have your salary continued——

THE KING.

Thank you, brother, I need your bounty no longer.

KING PIETRO.

Are you out of your senses?!

THE KING.

I see more clearly than you. You no more than I can prevent the wonderful fulfilment of mighty fate.

KING PIETRO.

Stop your idle babble! I ask you for the last time, will you obey my order? If not, fear my wrath!

THE KING.

It is beyond your power as well as mine!

KING PIETRO.

Very well. My son if he wants may run after you. I banish you and your child for life from this day forth from the land of Umbria, under pain of death in case you return to it!

THE KING.

(*Breaks forth in merry laughter.*)

FILIPO.

Holy Virgin, what's the matter with him!

KING PIETRO.

(*Disconcerted.*) It is the laughter of a madman.

THE KING.

(*Laughing.*) Surely, dear friends, you will permit me to laugh since I have been paid for being foolish.

KING PIETRO.

Give us some explanation of what is passing within you, Alexandrion!

THE KING.

(*Raising himself to his full height.*) Do you know that you banished me once before, in this very room, from Umbria under pain of death?!

KING PIETRO.

It is impossible fur me to remember all the judgments I have passed!

THE KING.

You passed your first judgment against King Nicola, and I am he!

KING PIETRO.

(*Shaken.*) It was long to be foreseen that he would come to such an end! (*To the King.*) Do you want to act a tragic scene for us out of your former occupation?

THE KING.

I, here before you, am King Nicola!

KING PIETRO.

(*With apparent anger.*) I have nothing to do with imposters. Do you really expect to gain your ends by such thieves' tricks?

THE KING.

I am King Nicola! I am King Nicola!

KING PIETRO.

(*To Filipo.*) He has had a stroke! God have mercy on his soul!

FILIPO.

His poor child! Merciful Heaven, when she hears of it!

THE KING.

(*In the greatest astonishment.*) Why are you not overcome with astonishment?——You do not believe me?!——Are you going to ask me to prove what since my downfall I have kept secret only by supernatural strength of soul!

FILIPO.

We believe you, Alexandrion! Let me conduct you to your room. We believe you!

KING PIETRO.

If only your poor heart would grow quiet!

THE KING.

(*Anxiously.*) No, no, I shall not grow quiet! You do not trust my words! You doubt my reason!——Almighty God, where shall I get witnesses to confirm the truth!——Let my daughter be called! It is high time; I shall not see the light much longer!——Let my daughter be called! I am too weak to fetch her myself.——Let my child be called!——My child!

FILIPO.

I beseech you, Father, do not gratify his wish! The girl will go crazy from anguish if unprepared she sees him in his mind's darkness!

THE KING.

Let my child be called! I have nothing to leave her but her princely ancestry, and now she is about to be cheated of this last possession through my stupendous folly! Who will believe the girl when my eyes are closed! Indeed, there is nothing in me to recall a king! And my pictures, my statues are destroyed! And even if a picture were found, who would accept a resemblance as proof of my monstrous statement! A resemblance in which time has destroyed every trace! Help me, Heavenly Father, in this anguish worse than death!

KING PIETRO.

Have you quite forgotten, my dear Alexandrion, that King Nicola is dead?!

THE KING.

Dead?———How kindly you speak because you think I am mad! Dead?——— Where is he buried? I fought against the flood and escaped to land beyond the city walls. But who will believe me! Call my child here! She will advise me, as she has done a hundred thousand times before, with her wisdom.

FILIPO.

I'll hurry and call your own physician, my respected father!

THE KING.

Call my child! My child!

PRINCESS ALMA.

(*Rushing in.*) My father! Almighty God, I heard your agonizing voice throughout the house!

THE KING.

Am I King Nicola, or am I not?

ALMA.

You are King Nicola, my father. Do not worry! What more can they do to us today?

THE KING.

So you too have gone mad or you are a miserable pretender! They don't believe us! What can we do to prove it to them, so that I may lay my head on the block and thereby give you attestation of your birth?! Send to the prison! There they have the record of the scars on my body. I blasphemed against the king. "Curse the king!" I cried. I was that king!———But where is a man with a normal reason who will believe such adventures! I never thought of that during all these years! Who would carry documents with him when his head had been twice forfeited to the executioner! And have I fathomed the ways of Almighty God more than anyone only to be considered mad in the end!——But such is life! Such is life!

KING PIETRO.

The sight of your sufferings is heartrending, Alexandrion! But your assertion is ridiculous!

ALMA.

He is King Nicola!

FILIPO.

Think what you say, Donna Alma!

ALMA.

He is King Nicola!

THE KING.

Search your brain, my dear, clever child, and see if you cannot find a means of making the truth shine before their eyes like a ray of sunshine!

ALMA. I will bring a host of witnesses, father, as soon as the penalty is taken off your head.

FILIPO.

Was not the name of King Nicola's daughter Alma?

KING PIETRO.

Thousands of children are baptized with princely names!

THE KING.

Do you hear, my child? An infallible proof! Otherwise, I shall yet end my unhappy war with the world in a madhouse and burden your life with the most gruesome of curses, the curse of the ridiculous!

ALMA.

Lead us to the Urselines!

FILIPO.

Can it be possible! The king in his victor's service! ——Speak, my father!——Pardon him!

KING PIETRO.

Be you who you may, I lift every penalty which may hang over you.

THE KING.

And now the proofs, my child! Quick, the proofs! Even if their testimony is as clear as day, it will do as little after my death to help the recognition of your birth as my vain words do now!

ALMA.

The Mother Superior of the Urselines will testify (*Frightened.*) My father! Jesu, Maria, your look! What are you seeking so helplessly? For God's sake, speak!

FILIPO.

(*Who has hurried to aid the King.*) Go, Donna Alma! The strength begins to leave his limbs.

THE KING.

(*Struggling against death, while Filipo and Alma support him upon the steps of the throne.*) I seek proofs!——Proofs! Who can prove by his corpse that he was a king!——It is the last chance!——I am not mad!——Hurry, my child!——Proofs!——Too late! too late!——Such is life!

ALMA.

(*Bending over him, lamenting.*) My father! Don't you hear me? Look me in the eye, my father! What is your hand seeking? Your child is kneeling beside you!

THE KING.

——I thank you, bu—but not as a king——only——as——a man——

ALMA.

Oh, oh, his eyes!——Father! Move your hand! Oh, woe is me, is there no help? Oh, pity me, he no longer hears my voice! His cheeks are cold! How can I warm his heart? Your mighty soul, my father, where is it, that it save you! Don't leave me alone, my father! Don't leave me alone! Oh, woe is me, woe is me, he has left me!

KING PIETRO.

(*To himself.*) I stand here like an outlaw!

FILIPO.

Quiet your sorrow, Donna Alma!

KING PIETRO.

I will seek to make amends for her loss to the best of my power, if she is willing to become my child through you.

FILIPO.

God bless you for that, my father!

KING PIETRO.

We will give him princely burial; whoever he may be! But nobody must hear a word of what we three have passed through here during this hour. History shall never tell of me that I made a king my court fool!

Curtain.